Contents

Acknowledgments

*The publisher would like to thank the companies and organizations
listed below for the use of their recipes and photographs in this publication.*

Dole Food Company, Inc.
Equal® sweetener
Hershey Food Corporation
SPLENDA® is a trademark of McNeil PPC, Inc.

PRESS

A division of Publications International, Ltd.

Rich Chocolate Cheesecake

1 cup chocolate wafer crumbs
3 tablespoons EQUAL® SPOONFUL*
3 tablespoons stick butter or margarine, melted
3 packages (8 ounces each) reduced-fat cream cheese, softened
1¼ cups EQUAL® SPOONFUL**
2 eggs
2 egg whites
2 tablespoons cornstarch
¼ teaspoon salt
1 cup reduced-fat sour cream
2 teaspoons vanilla
4 ounces (4 squares) semi-sweet chocolate, melted and slightly cooled

*May substitute 4½ packets Equal® sweetener.

**May substitute 30 packets Equal® sweetener.

• Mix chocolate crumbs, 3 tablespoons Equal® Spoonful and melted butter in bottom of 9-inch springform pan. Pat mixture evenly onto bottom of pan. Bake in preheated 325°F oven 8 minutes. Cool on wire rack.

• Beat cream cheese and 1¼ cups Equal® Spoonful in large bowl until fluffy; beat in eggs, egg whites, cornstarch and salt. Beat in sour cream and vanilla until well blended. Gently fold in melted chocolate. Pour batter into crust.

• Bake in 325°F oven 40 to 45 minutes or until center is almost set. Remove cheesecake to wire rack. Gently run metal spatula around rim of pan to loosen cake. Let cheesecake cool completely; cover and refrigerate several hours or overnight before serving. To serve, remove side of springform pan. *Makes 16 servings*

Nutrients Per Serving					
Calories	217	Cholesterol	62mg	Carbohydrate	13g
Sodium	246mg	Protein	7g	Fiber	1g
Total fat	16g				

Rich Chocolate Cheesecake

Key Lime Tarts

¾ cup fat-free (skim) milk
6 tablespoons fresh lime juice
2 tablespoons cornstarch
½ cup cholesterol-free egg substitute
½ cup reduced-fat sour cream
12 packages sugar substitute *or* equivalent of ½ cup sugar
4 sheets phyllo dough*
   Butter-flavored nonstick cooking spray
¾ cup thawed frozen fat-free nondairy whipped topping
   Fresh raspberries (optional)

Cover with damp kitchen towel to prevent dough from drying out.

1. Combine milk, lime juice and cornstarch in medium saucepan. Cook over medium heat 2 to 3 minutes, stirring constantly until thick. Remove from heat.

2. Add egg substitute; whisk constantly for 30 seconds to allow egg substitute to cook. Stir in sour cream and sugar substitute; cover and refrigerate until cool.

3. Preheat oven to 350°F. Spray 8 (2½-inch) muffin cups with cooking spray; set aside.

4. Place 1 sheet of phyllo dough on cutting board; spray with cooking spray. Top with second sheet of phyllo dough; spray with cooking spray. Top with third sheet of phyllo dough; spray with cooking spray. Top with last sheet; spray with cooking spray.

5. Cut stack of phyllo dough into 8 squares. Gently fit each stacked square into prepared muffin cup; press firmly against bottom and side. Bake 8 to 10 minutes or until golden brown. Carefully remove from muffin cups; cool on wire rack.

6. Divide lime mixture evenly among phyllo cups; top with whipped topping. Garnish with fresh raspberries, if desired.

Makes 8 servings

Nutrients Per Serving					
Calories	82	Cholesterol	5mg	Carbohydrate	13g
Sodium	88mg	Protein	3g	Fiber	<1g
Total fat	1g				

Key Lime Tarts

Cranberry Orange Cheesecake

1⅓ cups gingersnap crumbs
   3 tablespoons EQUAL® SPOONFUL*
   3 tablespoons stick butter or margarine, melted
   3 packages (8 ounces each) reduced-fat cream cheese, softened
   1 cup EQUAL® SPOONFUL**
   2 eggs
   2 egg whites
   2 tablespoons cornstarch
   ¼ teaspoon salt
   1 cup reduced-fat sour cream
   2 teaspoons vanilla
   1 cup chopped fresh or frozen cranberries
1½ teaspoons grated orange peel

May substitute 4½ packets Equal® sweetener.

**May substitute 24 packets Equal® sweetener.*

• Mix gingersnap crumbs, 3 tablespoons Equal® Spoonful and melted butter in bottom of 9-inch springform pan. Reserve 2 tablespoons crumb mixture. Pat remaining mixture evenly onto bottom of pan. Bake in preheated 325°F oven 8 minutes. Cool on wire rack.

• Beat cream cheese and 1 cup Equal® Spoonful in large bowl until fluffy; beat in eggs, egg whites, cornstarch and salt. Beat in sour cream and vanilla until blended. Gently stir in cranberries and orange peel. Pour batter into crust in pan. Sprinkle with reserved crumb mixture.

• Bake in 325°F oven 45 to 50 minutes or until center is almost set. Remove cheesecake to wire rack. Gently run metal spatula around rim of pan to loosen cake. Let cheesecake cool completely; cover and refrigerate several hours or overnight before serving. To serve, remove sides of springform pan.   *Makes 16 servings*

Nutrients Per Serving					
Calories	**196**	Cholesterol	**62mg**	Carbohydrate	**13g**
Sodium	**268mg**	Protein	**7g**	Fiber	**1g**
Total fat	**13g**				

Currant Cheesecake Bars

½ cup (1 stick) butter, softened
1 cup all-purpose flour
½ cup packed light brown sugar
½ cup finely chopped pecans
1 package (8 ounces) cream cheese, softened
¼ cup granulated sugar
1 egg
1 tablespoon milk
2 teaspoons grated lemon peel
⅓ cup currant jelly or seedless raspberry jam

Preheat oven to 350°F. Grease 9-inch square baking pan. Beat butter in medium bowl with electric mixer at medium speed until smooth. Add flour, brown sugar and pecans; beat at low speed until well blended. Press mixture into bottom and partially up sides of prepared pan.

Bake about 15 minutes or until light brown. If sides of crust have shrunk down, press back up and reshape with spoon. Let cool 5 minutes on wire rack.

Meanwhile, beat cream cheese in large bowl with electric mixer at medium speed until smooth. Add granulated sugar, egg, milk and lemon peel; beat until well blended.

Heat jelly in small saucepan over low heat 2 to 3 minutes or until smooth, stirring occasionally.

Pour cream cheese mixture over crust. Drizzle jelly in 7 to 8 horizontal strips across filling with spoon. Swirl jelly through filling with knife to create marbled effect.

Bake 20 to 25 minutes or until filling is set. Cool completely on wire rack before cutting into bars. Store in airtight container in refrigerator up to 1 week.   *Makes about 32 bars*

Nutrients Per Serving					
Calories	**105**	Cholesterol	**22mg**	Carbohydrate	**11g**
Sodium	**54mg**	Protein	**1g**	Fiber	**<1g**
Total fat	**7g**				

Pineapple-Ginger Bavarian

1 can (8 ounces) crushed pineapple in juice, drained and liquid
    reserved
1 package (4-serving size) sugar-free orange gelatin
1 cup sugar-free ginger ale
1 cup plain nonfat yogurt
¾ teaspoon grated fresh ginger
½ cup whipping cream
1 packet sugar substitute
¼ teaspoon vanilla

1. Combine reserved pineapple juice with enough water to equal
½ cup liquid. Pour into small saucepan. Bring to a boil over high heat.

2. Place gelatin in medium bowl. Add pineapple juice mixture; stir
until gelatin is completely dissolved. Add ginger ale and half of crushed
pineapple; stir until well blended. Add yogurt; whisk until well blended.
Pour into 5 individual ramekins. Cover each ramekin with plastic wrap;
refrigerate until firm.

3. Meanwhile, combine remaining half of pineapple with ginger in
small bowl. Cover with plastic wrap; refrigerate.

4. Just before serving, beat cream in small deep bowl on high speed
of electric mixer until soft peaks form. Add sugar substitute and vanilla;
beat until stiff peaks form.

5. To serve, top bavarian with 1 tablespoon whipped topping and
1 tablespoon pineapple mixture. *Makes 5 servings*

Tip: To save time, use 2 tablespoons ready-made whipped topping to
garnish.

Nutrients Per Serving					
Calories	**147**	Cholesterol	**34mg**	Carbohydrate	**12g**
Sodium	**111mg**	Protein	**4g**	Fiber	**<1g**
Total fat	**9g**				

Pineapple-Ginger Bavarian

Chocolate Swirled Cheesecake

   Yogurt Cheese (recipe follows)
2 tablespoons graham cracker crumbs
1 package (8 ounces) Neufchâtel cheese (⅓ less fat cream cheese),
   softened
1½ teaspoons vanilla extract
¾ cup sugar
1 tablespoon cornstarch
1 container (8 ounces) liquid egg substitute
¼ cup HERSHEY'S Cocoa
¼ teaspoon almond extract

1. Prepare Yogurt Cheese.

2. Heat oven to 325°F. Spray bottom of 8- or 9-inch springform pan with vegetable cooking spray. Sprinkle graham cracker crumbs on bottom of pan.

3. Beat Yogurt Cheese, Neufchâtel cheese and vanilla in large bowl on medium speed of mixer until smooth. Add sugar and cornstarch; beat just until well blended. Gradually add egg substitute, beating on low speed until blended.

4. Transfer 1½ cups batter to medium bowl; add cocoa. Beat until well blended. Stir almond extract into vanilla batter. Alternately spoon vanilla and chocolate batters into prepared pan. With knife or metal spatula, cut through batters for marble effect.

5. Bake 35 minutes for 8-inch pan, 40 minutes for 9-inch pan or until edge is set. With knife, loosen cheesecake from side of pan. Cool completely in pan on wire rack.

6. Cover; refrigerate at least 6 hours before serving. Just before serving, remove side of pan. Garnish as desired. Cover; refrigerate leftover cheesecake.   *Makes 16 servings*

Yogurt Cheese: Use one 16-ounce container plain lowfat yogurt, no gelatin added. Line non-rusting colander or sieve with large piece of double thickness cheesecloth or large coffee filter; place colander over deep bowl. Spoon yogurt into prepared colander; cover with plastic wrap. Refrigerate until liquid no longer drains from yogurt, about 24 hours. Remove yogurt from cheesecloth and place in separate bowl; discard liquid.

continued on page 14

Chocolate Swirled Cheesecake

Chocolate Swirled Cheesecake, continued

Nutrients Per Serving					
Calories	**110**	Cholesterol	**15mg**	Carbohydrate	**12g**
Sodium	**100mg**	Protein	**4g**	Fiber	**<1g**
Total fat	**4g**				

Easy Fruit Tarts

12 **wonton skins**
   Vegetable cooking spray
 2 **tablespoons apple jelly or apricot fruit spread**
1½ **cups sliced or cut-up fruit such as DOLE® Bananas, Strawberries**
      or Red or Green Seedless Grapes
 1 **cup nonfat or low fat yogurt, any flavor**

• Press wonton skins into 12 muffin cups sprayed with vegetable cooking spray, allowing corners to stand up over edges of muffin cups.

• Bake at 375°F 5 minutes or until lightly browned. Carefully remove wonton cups to wire rack; cool.

• Cook and stir jelly in small saucepan over low heat until jelly melts.

• Brush bottoms of cooled wonton cups with melted jelly. Place two fruit slices in each cup; spoon rounded tablespoon of yogurt on top of fruit. Garnish with fruit slice and mint leaves. Serve immediately.

Makes 12 servings

Prep Time: 20 minutes
Bake Time: 5 minutes

Nutrients Per Serving					
Calories	**57**	Cholesterol	**2mg**	Carbohydrate	**12g**
Sodium	**32mg**	Protein	**1g**	Fiber	**1g**
Total fat	**<1g**				

Double Chocolate Brownies

1 cup EQUAL® SPOONFUL*
¾ cup all-purpose flour
½ cup semi-sweet chocolate chips or mini chocolate chips
6 tablespoons unsweetened cocoa powder
1 teaspoon baking powder
¼ teaspoon salt
6 tablespoons stick butter or margarine, softened
½ cup unsweetened applesauce
2 eggs
1 teaspoon vanilla

*May substitute 24 packets Equal® sweetener.

• Combine Equal®, flour, chocolate chips, cocoa, baking powder and salt. Beat butter, applesauce, eggs and vanilla until blended. Stir in flour mixture until blended.

• Spread batter in 8-inch square baking pan sprayed with nonstick cooking spray. Bake in preheated 350°F oven 18 to 20 minutes or until top springs back when gently touched. Cool completely on wire rack.

Makes 16 servings

Nutrients Per Serving					
Calories	**108**	Cholesterol	**38mg**	Carbohydrate	**10g**
Sodium	**119mg**	Protein	**2g**	Fiber	**1g**
Total fat	**7g**				

Smart Tip

Unsweetened cocoa is formed by extracting
most of the cocoa butter from pure chocolate
and grinding the remaining chocolate solids
into a powder. Since cocoa powder is
naturally lower in fat than other chocolate
baking ingredients, it is often used to
make reduced-fat baked goods.

Cool Lime Cheesecake

1 cup graham cracker crumbs
3 tablespoons stick butter or margarine, melted
2 tablespoons EQUAL® SPOONFUL*
2 packages (8 ounces each) reduced-fat cream cheese, softened
⅔ cup EQUAL® SPOONFUL**
1 egg
2 egg whites
½ teaspoon grated lime peel
3 tablespoons fresh lime juice

*May substitute 3 packets Equal® sweetener.

**May substitute 16 packets Equal® sweetener.

• Combine graham cracker crumbs, melted butter and 2 tablespoons Equal® Spoonful in bottom of 8-inch springform pan or 8-inch cake pan; pat evenly on bottom and ½ inch up side of pan. Bake in preheated 325°F oven 8 minutes.

• Beat cream cheese and ⅔ cup Equal® Spoonful in medium bowl until fluffy. Beat in egg, egg whites, lime peel and juice until well blended. Pour cream cheese mixture into prepared crust.

• Bake in 325°F oven 30 to 35 minutes or until center is almost set. Cool on wire rack. Refrigerate at least 3 hours before serving.

Makes 8 servings

Nutrients Per Serving					
Calories	**197**	Cholesterol	**58mg**	Carbohydrate	**14g**
Sodium	**366mg**	Protein	**9g**	Fiber	**<1g**
Total fat	**11g**				

Smart Tip

When using both the juice and peel of a lime or lemon, grate the peel first, then squeeze the juice. One medium lime will yield about 1½ tablespoons juice and 1½ teaspoons grated peel.

Cool Lime Cheesecake

Chocolate-Almond Meringue Puffs

2 tablespoons granulated sugar
3 packages sugar substitute
1½ teaspoons unsweetened cocoa powder
2 egg whites, at room temperature
½ teaspoon vanilla
¼ teaspoon cream of tartar
¼ teaspoon almond extract
⅛ teaspoon salt
1½ ounces sliced almonds
3 tablespoons sugar-free seedless raspberry fruit spread

1. Preheat oven to 275°F. Combine granulated sugar, sugar substitute and cocoa powder in small bowl; set aside.

2. Beat egg whites in small bowl on high speed of electric mixer until foamy. Add vanilla, cream of tartar, almond extract and salt; beat until soft peaks form. Add sugar mixture, 1 tablespoon at a time, beating until stiff peaks form.

3. Line baking sheet with foil. Spoon 15 equal mounds of egg white mixture onto foil. Sprinkle with almonds.

4. Bake 1 hour. Turn oven off but do not open oven door. Leave puffs in oven 2 hours longer or until completely dry. Remove from oven; cool completely.

5. Stir fruit spread and spoon about ½ teaspoon onto each meringue just before serving.   *Makes 15 cookies*

Tip: Cookies are best if eaten the same day they're made. If necessary, store in airtight container, adding fruit topping at time of serving.

Nutrients Per Serving					
Calories	**34**	Cholesterol	**0mg**	Carbohydrate	**4g**
Sodium	**27mg**	Protein	**1g**	Fiber	**<1g**
Total fat	**1g**				

Chocolate-Almond Meringue Puffs

Strawberry Bavarian Deluxe

½ bag whole frozen unsweetened strawberries
   (1 mounded quart), partially thawed
¼ cup low-sugar strawberry preserves
¼ cup granular sucralose
¾ cup water, divided
2 tablespoons balsamic vinegar
2 envelopes (7g each) unflavored gelatin
1 tablespoon honey
½ cup pasteurized liquid egg whites
½ teaspoon cream of tartar
1 teaspoon vanilla
1 pint strawberries, washed, dried and hulled
   Mint sprigs (optional)
1 cup thawed frozen light whipped topping

1. Place frozen strawberries, preserves and sucralose in bowl of food processor fitted with metal blade. Process until smooth. Transfer mixture to bowl. Set aside.

2. Combine ¼ cup water and vinegar in small saucepan. Sprinkle in gelatin and let stand until softened. Add remaining ½ cup water to saucepan with honey; stir to blend. Cook and stir over medium heat until gelatin dissolves.

3. Whisk gelatin mixture into berry mixture in bowl. Refrigerate, covered, until mixture is soupy, but not set.

4. Meanwhile, combine liquid egg whites and cream of tartar in bowl. When berry-gelatin mixture is soupy, whip egg white mixture and vanilla until tripled in volume and at soft peak stage.

5. Gently fold egg whites, ⅓ at a time, into chilled berry-gelatin mixture, being careful not to deflate egg whites. Fold until mixture is uniform color. Scrape mixture into prechilled 2-quart mold, such as a nonstick Bundt pan. Cover and refrigerate at least 8 hours or overnight.

6. To serve, run tip of knife around top of mold, inside rim and center (if using Bundt pan). Dip mold briefly into large bowl of hot water to loosen mousse, lifting occasionally and shaking gently to see if mousse is released. To unmold, center flat serving plate on top of mold, hold firmly so mold doesn't shift, and invert plate and mold. Shake gently to release.

Remove mold and refrigerate. After 10 to 15 minutes, remove from refrigerator and garnish with fresh strawberries and mint sprigs, if desired. Cut into wedges and serve with whipped topping.

Makes 10 servings

Nutrients Per Serving					
Calories	**82**	Cholesterol	**0mg**	Carbohydrate	**15g**
Sodium	**25mg**	Protein	**3g**	Fiber	**2g**
Total fat	**1g**				

Holiday Thumbprint Cookies

1 **package (8 ounces) sugar-free low-fat yellow cake mix**
3 **tablespoons orange juice**
2 **teaspoons grated orange peel**
½ **teaspoon vanilla**
5 **teaspoons strawberry all-fruit spread**
2 **tablespoons pecans, chopped**

1. Preheat oven to 350°F. Spray baking sheets with nonstick cooking spray.

2. Beat cake mix, orange juice, orange peel and vanilla in medium bowl with electric mixer at medium speed 2 minutes or until mixture looks crumbly. Increase speed to medium and beat 2 minutes or until smooth dough forms. (Dough will be very sticky.)

3. Coat hands with nonstick cooking spray. Roll dough into 1-inch balls. Place balls 2½ inches apart on prepared baking sheets. Press center of each ball with thumb. Fill each thumbprint with ¼ teaspoon fruit spread. Sprinkle with nuts.

4. Bake 8 to 9 minutes or until cookies are light golden brown and lose their shininess. *Do not overbake.* Remove to wire racks; cool completely.

Makes 20 cookies

Nutrients Per Serving					
Calories	**50**	Cholesterol	**0mg**	Carbohydrate	**10g**
Sodium	**8mg**	Protein	**1g**	Fiber	**0g**
Total fat	**1g**				

Apple-Cranberry Crescent Cookies

1¼ cups chopped apples
½ cup dried cranberries
½ cup reduced-fat sour cream
¼ cup cholesterol-free egg substitute
¼ cup margarine or butter, melted
3 tablespoons sugar, divided
1 package quick-rise active dry yeast
1 teaspoon vanilla
2 cups all-purpose flour
1 teaspoon ground cinnamon
1 tablespoon reduced-fat (2%) milk

1. Preheat oven to 350°F. Lightly coat cookie sheet with nonstick cooking spray.

2. Place apples and cranberries in food processor or blender; pulse to finely chop. Set aside.

3. Combine sour cream, egg substitute, margarine and 2 tablespoons sugar in medium bowl. Add yeast and vanilla. Add flour; stir to form ball. Turn dough out onto lightly floured work surface. Knead 1 minute. Cover with plastic wrap; allow to stand 10 minutes.

4. Divide dough into thirds. Roll one portion into 12-inch circle. Spread with ⅓ apple mixture (about ¼ cup). Cut dough to make 8 wedges. Roll up each wedge, beginning at outside edge. Place on prepared cookie sheet; turn ends of cookies to form crescents. Repeat with remaining dough and apple mixture.

5. Combine remaining 1 tablespoon sugar and cinnamon in small bowl. Lightly brush cookies with milk; sprinkle with sugar-cinnamon mixture. Bake cookies 18 to 20 minutes or until lightly browned.

Makes 2 dozen cookies

Nutrients Per Serving					
Calories	**82**	Cholesterol	**2mg**	Carbohydrate	**13g**
Sodium	**31mg**	Protein	**2g**	Fiber	**1g**
Total fat	**2g**				

Apple-Cranberry Crescent Cookies

Peanut Butter Chocolate Bars

1 cup EQUAL® SPOONFUL*
½ cup (1 stick) butter or margarine, softened
⅓ cup firmly packed brown sugar
½ cup 2% milk
½ cup creamy peanut butter
1 egg
1 teaspoon vanilla
1 cup all-purpose flour
1 cup quick oats, uncooked
½ teaspoon baking soda
¼ teaspoon salt
¾ cup mini semi-sweet chocolate chips

May substitute 24 packets Equal® sweetener.

• Beat Equal®, butter and brown sugar until well combined. Stir in milk, peanut butter, egg and vanilla until blended. Gradually mix in combined flour, oats, baking soda and salt until blended. Stir in chocolate chips.

• Spread mixture evenly in 13×9-inch baking pan generously coated with nonstick cooking spray. Bake in preheated 350°F oven 20 to 22 minutes. Cool completely in pan on wire rack. Cut into squares; store in airtight container at room temperature.   *Makes 48 bars*

Nutrients Per Serving					
Calories	75	Cholesterol	10mg	Carbohydrate	8g
Sodium	60mg	Protein	1g	Fiber	1g
Total fat	5g				

Peanut Butter Chocolate Bars

Watermelon Ice

4 cups seeded 1-inch watermelon chunks
¼ cup thawed frozen unsweetened pineapple juice concentrate
2 tablespoons fresh lime juice
　Fresh melon balls (optional)
　Fresh mint leaves (optional)

Place melon chunks in single layer in plastic freezer bag; freeze until firm, about 8 hours. Place frozen melon in food processor container fitted with steel blade. Let stand 15 minutes to soften slightly. Add pineapple juice and lime juice. Remove plunger from top of food processor to allow air to be incorporated. Process until smooth, scraping down side of container frequently. Spoon into individual dessert dishes. Garnish with melon balls and mint leaves, if desired. Freeze leftovers.

Makes 6 servings

Honeydew Ice: Substitute honeydew for watermelon and unsweetened pineapple-guava-orange juice concentrate for pineapple juice concentrate.

Cantaloupe Ice: Substitute cantaloupe for watermelon and unsweetened pineapple-guava-orange juice concentrate for pineapple juice concentrate.

Note: Ices may be transferred to airtight container and frozen up to 1 month. Let stand at room temperature 10 minutes to soften slightly before serving.

Nutrients Per Serving					
Calories	**57**	Cholesterol	**0mg**	Carbohydrate	**13g**
Sodium	**3mg**	Protein	**1g**	Fiber	**1g**
Total fat	**<1g**				

Raspberry Cheese Tarts

Crust
  1¼ **cups graham cracker crumbs**
    5 **tablespoons light margarine (50% less fat and calories)**
  ¼ **cup SPLENDA® Granular**

Filling
    4 **ounces reduced-fat cream cheese**
  ½ **cup plain nonfat yogurt**
    1 **cup SPLENDA® Granular**
  ½ **cup egg substitute**
    1 **cup frozen raspberries**

Crust

1. Preheat oven to 350°F. In medium bowl, mix graham cracker crumbs, margarine and ¼ cup SPLENDA®. Press about 1 tablespoon crust mixture into each of 10 muffin pan cups lined with paper liners. Set aside.

Filling

2. In small bowl, beat cream cheese with electric mixer on low speed until soft, about 30 seconds. Add yogurt and beat on low speed until smooth, about 1 minute. Stir in 1 cup SPLENDA® and egg substitute until well blended.

3. Place 1½ tablespoons raspberries (4 to 5) in each muffin cup. Divide filling evenly among muffin cups. Bake for 20 minutes or until firm.

4. Refrigerate for 2 hours before serving. Garnish as desired.

Makes 10 servings

Prep Time: 25 minutes
Bake Time: 20 minutes
Chill Time: 2 hours

Nutrients Per Serving					
Calories	**140**	Cholesterol	**6mg**	Carbohydrate	**15g**
Sodium	**255mg**	Protein	**5g**	Fiber	**1g**
Total fat	**6g**				

Strawberry-Topped Cheesecake Cups

1 cup sliced strawberries
10 packages sugar substitute, divided
1 teaspoon vanilla, divided
½ teaspoon grated orange peel
¼ teaspoon grated fresh ginger
1 package (8 ounces) cream cheese, softened
½ cup sour cream
2 tablespoons granulated sugar
16 vanilla wafers, crushed
Fresh mint leaves (optional)

1. Combine strawberries, 1 package sugar substitute, ¼ teaspoon vanilla, orange peel and grated ginger in medium bowl; toss gently. Let stand 20 minutes to allow flavors to blend.

2. Meanwhile, combine cream cheese, sour cream, remaining 9 packets sugar substitute and granulated sugar in medium mixing bowl. Add remaining ¾ teaspoon vanilla; beat 30 seconds on low speed of electric mixer. Increase to medium speed; beat 30 seconds or until smooth.

3. Spoon cream cheese mixture into 8 individual ¼-cup ramekins. Top each with about 2 tablespoons vanilla wafer crumbs and about 2 tablespoons strawberry mixture. Garnish with mint, if desired.

Makes 8 servings

Nutrients Per Serving					
Calories	**205**	Cholesterol	**36mg**	Carbohydrate	**15g**
Sodium	**127mg**	Protein	**3g**	Fiber	**<1g**
Total fat	**15g**				

Strawberry-Topped Cheesecake Cups

Frozen Berry Ice Cream

8 ounces frozen unsweetened strawberries, partially thawed
8 ounces frozen unsweetened peaches, partially thawed
4 ounces frozen unsweetened blueberries, partially thawed
6 packets sugar substitute
2 teaspoons vanilla
2 cups no-sugar-added light vanilla ice cream
16 blueberries
4 small strawberries, halved
8 peach slices

In food processor, combine frozen strawberries, peaches, blueberries, sugar substitute and vanilla. Process until coarsely chopped. Add ice cream; process until well blended.

Serve immediately for semi-soft texture or freeze until needed and allow to stand 10 minutes to soften slightly. Garnish each serving with 2 blueberries for "eyes," 1 strawberry half for "nose" and 1 peach slice for "smile."   *Makes 8 servings (½ cup each)*

Nutrients Per Serving					
Calories	69	Cholesterol	0mg	Carbohydrate	15g
Sodium	23mg	Protein	3g	Fiber	1g
Total fat	<1g				

Chocolate-Peanut Butter-Apple Treats

½ (8-ounce package) fat-free or reduced-fat cream cheese, softened
¼ cup reduced-fat chunky peanut butter
2 tablespoons mini chocolate chips
2 large apples

1. Combine cream cheese, peanut butter and chocolate chips in small bowl; mix well.

2. Cut each apple into 12 wedges; discard stems and seeds. Spread about 1½ teaspoons of the mixture over each apple wedge.

Makes 6 servings

Nutrients Per Serving					
Calories	101	Cholesterol	2mg	Carbohydrate	12g
Sodium	144mg	Protein	4g	Fiber	2g
Total fat	4g				